Moreno Valley
Public Library
25480 Alessandro Blvd.
Moreno Valley, CA 92553

April 24, 2014

Getting To Know...

Nature's Children

Monarch Butterflies

Bill Ivy

SCHOLASTIC INC.

New York   Toronto   London   Auckland   Sydney
Mexico City   New Delhi   Hong Kong   Buenos Aires

Facts in Brief

Classification of the Monarch Butterfly

     Class: *Insecta* (insects)
     Order: *Lepidoptera* (butterflies)
     Family: *Danaidae* (milkweed butterfly family)
     Genus: *Danaus*
     Species: *Danaus plexippus*

World distribution. North, South, and Central America; Europe; and Australia.

Habitat. Require warm sunny weather and access to the milkweed plant.

Distinctive physical characteristics. Orange wings with black lines and a black border with rows of small white spots.

Habits. Slow deliberate flight; active in daytime; lays eggs on milkweed plant; migrates in large swarms for the winter to southern United States, Mexico, and Central America.

Diet. Nectar of flowers, preferably milkweed blooms.

Published by Scholastic Inc.
90 Old Sherman Turnpike, Danbury, Connecticut 06816.

SCHOLASTIC and associated logos are trademarks and/or registered trademarks of Scholastic Inc.

ISBN: 0-7172-6065-8   Printed in the U.S.A.

Edited by: Elizabeth Grace Zuraw   *Photo Editor:* Nancy Norton
Photo Rights: Ivy Images   *Cover Design:* Niemand Design

Have you ever wondered . . .

If you sit quietly by a flower garden on a summer afternoon, you might be lucky enough to see a butterfly. It's probably looking for food in the flowers.

There are thousands of different kinds of butterflies in the world. Some are almost as big as dinner plates. Others are brilliantly colored. Still others, such as the Swallowtail, have long, slender "tails."

Butterflies may come in a wide variety of shapes, colors, and sizes, but they all have one thing in common. They all go through four stages in their lives. People go through stages, too—we all start life as babies, grow into children and then teenagers, and finally become adults. But through all of these stages, we don't change completely; we just get bigger.

A butterfly, however, looks *very* different in each stage of its life. It starts out as a tiny egg and hatches into a many-legged caterpillar. The caterpillar then curls up and wraps itself with a thin covering. When it finally breaks out of this "shell," it's a beautiful flying creature—a butterfly.

Opposite page: *The elegant Monarch Butterfly is always a delight to see.*

The Royal Butterfly

Most people agree that the lion is the King of Beasts. But do you know who is king of the butterfly world? It's the Monarch, of course, as its very name suggests.

And no wonder the Monarch Butterfly is considered the king of butterflies. Its paper-thin wings may be fragile and delicate, yet some Monarchs perform the incredible feat of flying the length of North America in their short lifetimes.

And long-distance flying is just one part of the Monarch's amazing life story. Let's follow this fascinating butterfly through some of the other facets of its life.

The Monarch, like most butterflies, comes out during the day. But moths, close relatives of butterflies, come out at night.

Milkweed Muncher

If you have milkweed plants near your house, you probably also have Monarch Butterflies. The Monarch depends on the milkweed for food as well as a place to lay its eggs.

Wherever milkweed grows, the Monarch soon follows. Long ago, Monarch Butterflies were found only in North, South, and Central America, but now they also live in Europe and Australia. No one knows how the Monarch managed to cross the oceans, but we do know that when the milkweed plant spread to new countries, so did the Monarch.

The milkweed plant commonly has rose or lavender flowers and leaves and stems that ooze a thick milky juice when they're cut or broken.

Small Beginnings

The Monarch Butterfly begins its life as a tiny egg no bigger than the head of a pin. When the female butterfly is ready to lay her eggs, she carefully searches for suitable milkweed plants. She chooses only young, healthy plants. She knows that the caterpillars that will soon hatch from the eggs will need fresh, tender leaves to eat.

The mother Monarch lays her eggs one by one on the underside of milkweed leaves. When she's done, she will have laid about 400 eggs.

You'd have to look hard to see a newly laid Monarch egg because its creamy yellow color blends in with the pale green milkweed leaf. As the caterpillar grows inside it, the egg changes color. It becomes yellow, then light gray, and finally dark gray. At last the shiny black head of the newly formed caterpillar can be seen through the eggshell. Four days to a week after the Monarch egg is laid, the caterpillar chews a hole through the shell and slowly crawls out. It's so tiny it's barely visible to the naked eye.

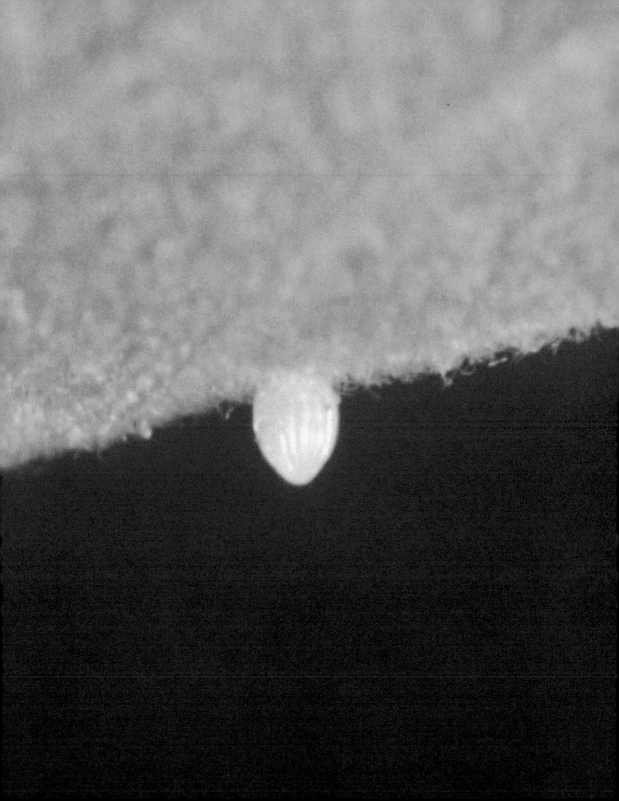

The Eating Machine

Although the newly hatched caterpillar, called a *larva,* is tiny—not even one-eighth inch (less than 3 millimeters) long—it has a huge appetite. First it eats its own eggshell, then the caterpillar begins to feed on the milkweed plant. This miniature eating machine eats day and night, stopping briefly only to rest between meals. It can eat a whole milkweed leaf in just four minutes! During the first day of its life, the caterpillar eats its own weight in food. Soon it is twice as big as when it hatched. If an average-size newborn human baby ate at the same rate, it would weigh about eight tons in 12 days!

In two weeks' time, the tiny, newly hatched caterpillar shown at the bottom of the photo will be full-grown.

Caterpillar Close-up

For two weeks, all the caterpillar does is eat. The yellow, black, and white Monarch caterpillar grows to a length of 2 inches (5 centimeters) and weighs 2,700 times more than when it hatched!

During this time, the caterpillar grows so fast that it keeps outgrowing its skin. Every three or four days it has to *molt,* or shed its skin. Each time it molts, it reveals a newer and brighter layer of skin that's been growing underneath. And after each molting, even more yellow and black stripes are revealed.

A caterpillar's body ends up with 13 ring-like sections. Instead of a nose, the caterpillar breathes through holes in these sections. These breathing holes, called *spiracles,* look like the portholes along the side of a ship.

On the underside of the caterpillar's body are six small legs and five pairs of *claspers*—small hooklike claws—that the caterpillar uses for gripping and moving along stems and leaves. It's hard to believe that this wormlike creature will one day become a beautiful butterfly.

Opposite page:
A caterpillar's life isn't just one long happy food fest. There's always the danger of being spotted by hungry birds and other enemies. And a tiny new caterpillar can easily drown in a drop of water.

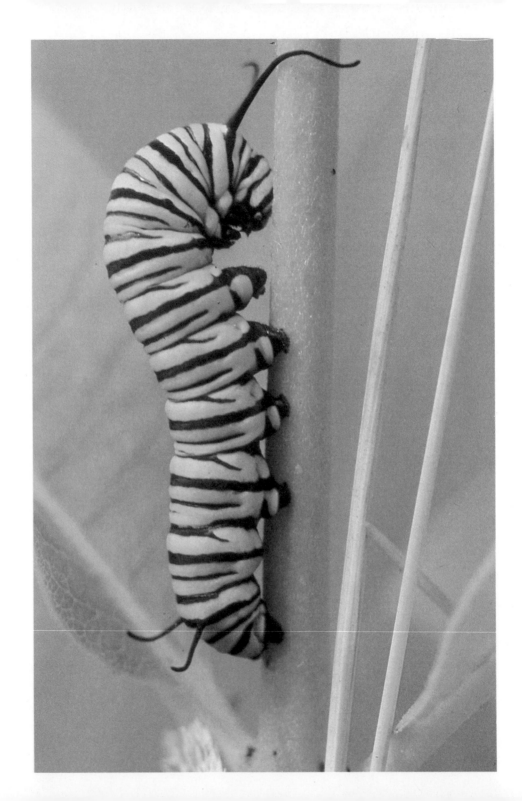

Heads or Tails?

You might have trouble telling the caterpillar's head from its tail. Both the head and tail have long, black growths on them that resemble antennae. But if you looked closely at these dark *filaments,* or threadlike structures, you'd see that one set of them is longer than the other. The longer ones are on the caterpillar's head. The shorter ones are on its tail.

The caterpillar uses the filaments to help fight off *predators,* animals that hunt other insects and animals for food. The filaments may also help the caterpillar feel its way around, and they're also useful for swishing away pesky flies that try to lay their eggs on the caterpillar's back.

Which end is up? The caterpillar's head is at the top of the photo—those filaments are longer than the ones at the bottom end.

Talented Tail

Having a tail that looks like a head is useful to the caterpillar. It confuses birds, mice, and other animals that like to eat caterpillars, just as it might have confused you. To avoid being eaten, the caterpillar wiggles its tail at predators. This protects the caterpillar's head by drawing attention to its tail, where a bite will cause less damage.

If these defenses don't work, the Monarch caterpillar may drop off its milkweed plant onto the ground. There it will play dead until the danger is passed. Then the caterpillar will often climb back up onto the same milkweed and continue its eating marathon.

The Monarch caterpillar often hangs upside down while enjoying a tasty meal of milkweed.

Preparing for Change

Even after they're fully grown, Monarch caterpillars continue to eat voraciously. They're preparing for an amazing series of changes that will soon transform them from slow-moving caterpillars to beautiful, brightly colored, darting butterflies.

The first signal of the changes to come is that the caterpillars become very restless. Some leave the milkweed plants that have been their home since hatching. They wander for as long as two days, looking for a safe place to continue their amazing transformation. Most choose a spot high off the ground so that they're out of reach of hungry field mice or other insect-eaters.

Once it has found a safe spot, the caterpillar uses its *spinneret,* a special body part in its mouth, to produce some sticky silky threads. These are woven into a small silk button underneath a twig or leaf. Then the caterpillar turns around and uses a little hook near its rear legs to attach itself to the silk button. Attached in that way, the caterpillar swings free and hangs upside down in the shape of the letter *J.* What will happen next?

Opposite page: *Hanging by its tail from a small sticky silk button it has spun, the caterpillar is now ready for the next stage of its development.*

The Little Green House

The caterpillar begins to move, arching its back to force the skin to split open. Then it wriggles for up to five hours to shed its skin for the last time. When its old skin is gone, the caterpillar looks like a large green drop of water. It has entered its *pupa* stage.

No longer a caterpillar but not yet a butterfly, this large green drop slowly begins to change shape and color. Its outer layer starts to harden into an elegant green, lantern-like case decorated with gold dots. The case is known as a *chrysalis* (KRISS-uh-liss), a name that comes from the Greek word for "golden." The Monarch's little green house with the single ring of golden dots around it hangs perfectly still, but inside, amazing things are happening.

Shedding its skin for the last time, this Monarch caterpillar is entering its pupa stage. Pupa *is a Latin word meaning "doll." The name was given to this stage of development because the chrysalis wraps itself around the form of the butterfly the way a blanket is wrapped around a baby or a doll.*

Monarch Magic

Inside the chrysalis, one of the great wonders of nature takes place. No one fully understands just how this miraculous change happens, but the body of the caterpillar is transformed into an adult butterfly.

All is quiet for nine to fifteen days. Then the chrysalis shell turns a rich teal blue and it gradually becomes totally transparent. The adult Monarch is now visible, with its miniature flame-colored wings and jet black body cramped inside. Hanging with its head down, the butterfly waits for the right moment to break out of its jeweled cage.

It's hard to believe that inside these "little green houses," caterpillars are getting ready to become butterflies.

A Brand New Butterfly

The Monarch Butterfly knows by *instinct,* a strong inborn urge, just the right moment to emerge from its chrysalis. It won't come out on a rainy or cool day because it must be warm for the butterfly to be active.

Usually the Monarch emerges on a bright sunny morning. The colorful case stirs and a tiny slit appears on the bottom of it. The chrysalis continues to rip open, and within two minutes a rumpled form tumbles out in a backward somersault and clings to the empty chrysalis.

A butterfly is born!

Taking Wing

The new butterfly has limp, crumpled wings that look like folded parachutes. Immediately they begin to unfold as the butterfly pumps them full of body fluid from its swollen body. It takes 20 minutes before its wings are full size.

Slowly the Monarch begins to sway back and forth and joins the two halves of its tongue together to form a tube. This is very important, for it is this tube that enables the Monarch to eat. Next the Monarch rests, waiting for the warmth of the sun to dry and harden its wings. Then, for the first time in its life, this royal butterfly rises up on delicate wings and flies.

It takes a few hours for the butterfly's wings to dry and harden. Until that happens, the butterfly cannot fly.

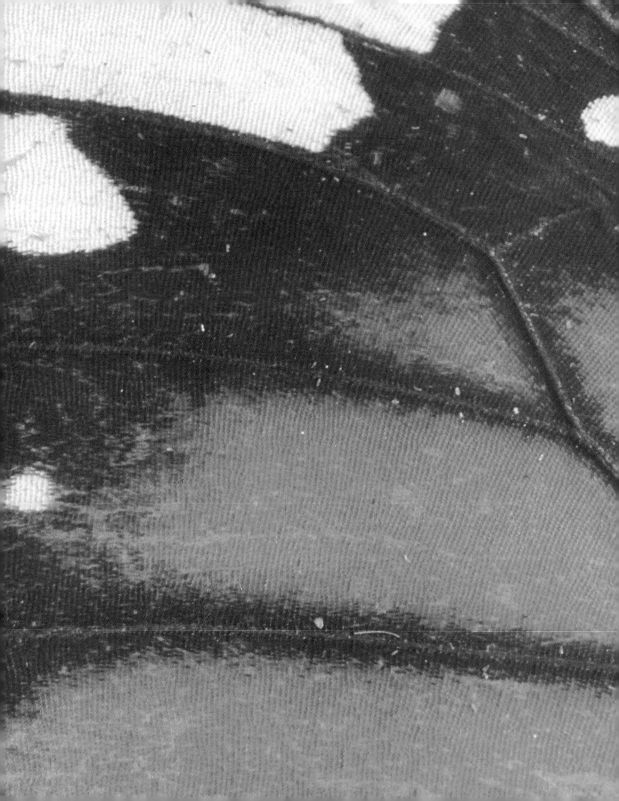

Meet the Monarch

The Monarch has two pairs of vividly patterned wings, covered with millions of tiny, colored scales. These overlap each other like shingles on a roof.

This is why the family name for butterflies is *Lepidoptera* (Leh-pih-DOP-teh-ruh), a Greek work that means "scale-winged." If you were to touch the Monarch's wings, these dainty flakes would rub off like fine powder onto your fingers.

Like all insects, the Monarch has six legs and three body sections: the head, thorax, and abdomen. But for some reason this butterfly doesn't seem to need all six of its legs. It always holds the front pair folded up close to its body.

The bright colors on the Monarch's wings are really layers of scales. Underneath the scales, the wings themselves are transparent.

Monarch Senses

It's hard to imagine using the soles of your feet for tasting food, but that's what a Monarch does. And the arrangement works very well for the butterfly. In fact, a Monarch's feet are much more sensitive to sweetness than your tongue is!

Stranger still are the Monarch's bulging eyes. They seem much too big for its head. But it's no wonder they're so big. Each large eye contains 6,000 lenses! A *lens* is a part of the eye that helps the eye see things. No one is sure how the world looks to a Monarch, but we do know that it can detect movement better than almost any other living creature. Just try to catch a butterfly!

Despite its superb eyesight, this butterfly relies even more on its sense of smell. The Monarch has two *antennae,* long sensitive feelers located between its eyes. The antennae act as the Monarch's nose and ears. They help direct the Monarch to its favorite flowers.

*This Monarch, like most butterflies, has
small knobs on the ends of its antennae.*

Flower Food

In less than a month, the Monarch has gone through four stages of life: egg, caterpillar, pupa, and adult butterfly. No more changes will take place in the Monarch's development, nor will the butterfly grow. But even though it has stopped growing, it still needs energy, so it must eat.

For its first three days as a butterfly, the Monarch feeds constantly. Instead of eating leaves as it did when it was a caterpillar, it now lives on the nectar of flowers. *Nectar* is the sweet juice produced by plants. It's the same sweet liquid bees use to make honey. The Monarch flits from flower to flower, using its hollow tongue, called a *proboscis* (pro-BAH-sis), to drink the nectar that forms in the blossoms of flowers. When not using this handy built-in straw, the butterfly coils it up under its head.

Like all butterflies, the Monarch uses taste sensors, located in its feet, to find and identify food.

A Happy Wanderer

After feasting for three days, the Monarch Butterfly drifts about over meadows and fields. It may travel great distances in its wanderings, sleeping in any handy tree or bush at night, and pausing at any handy flower for a meal when it gets hungry.

Although the Monarch needs the warmth of the sun and loves bright sunny weather, it's often seen flying just before a thunderstorm. For this reason, the Monarch is nicknamed the storm butterfly.

When the milkweed is in blossom, Monarchs will choose the milkweed's flowers over all others. But if none are around, any flower will do just fine.

Predators Beware!

Opposite page:
*Even though
Monarchs and
Viceroys are
look-alikes, one
way to tell them
apart is to look at
their hind wings.
The Viceroy has a
black line across
its hind wings; the
Monarch doesn't.*

The Monarch can fly up and out of the way of ground-dwelling predators, such as shrews and mice. And once it's airborne, it has an unusual way of defending itself against fast-flying birds. The Monarch has a bitter taste that can be poisonous to a bird if it swallows too much of the butterfly. The Monarch tastes this way because of chemicals in the milkweed plant that it ate as a caterpillar. Birds soon learn to avoid orange and black butterflies because they're not good food.

Another kind of butterfly, the Viceroy, makes good use of the Monarch's bird-proof taste. The Viceroy looks so much like a Monarch that birds leave it alone as well, even though they would probably find the Viceroy a tasty snack. The Viceroy's Monarch disguise is a very effective way of protecting itself from hungry birds.

Incredible Journey

Monarchs are the only insects that *migrate,* or travel each year in search of food or suitable climate. They fly to warm southern regions for the winter. The butterflies start out alone as soon as the northern autumn turns cold. But migrating butterflies may gather in large groups as they wait for good conditions at difficult crossing points. Many Monarchs will travel almost 2,000 miles (3,200 kilometers) before they reach their final destination.

The Monarchs travel by day at about the same speed as a fast jogger, occasionally stopping to feed. Just one feeding of nectar can keep them going for a week or more. With good winds pushing them, some have been known to travel 80 miles (about 130 kilometers) in a single day.

The Monarchs follow the same routes and perch in the same trees that generations of Monarchs have used before them. That's amazing because many of the butterflies have never migrated before. How they do this is yet another of the great mysteries of the Monarch.

Opposite page: While journeying to their winter grounds, these Monarchs take a rest by hooking their feet onto pine needles to stay securely attached.

40

Winter in the South

Try to imagine so many Monarch Butterflies that you can't see the bark of the trees that they're sitting on. You can't see any leaves or pine needles either—just Monarchs, Monarchs, everywhere. Some of these "butterfly trees" become so heavily laden with Monarchs that their branches may actually snap under the great weight!

Monarchs from eastern North America head for Mexico. Monarchs from western North America congregate in California along the Pacific coast. One of the most famous of the Monarch's wintering grounds is Pacific Grove, California. Each year, school children in that area hold a parade to celebrate the arrival of the Monarchs.

All winter long, the Monarchs rarely leave their "butterfly trees" except to feed. With the arrival of spring, however, they're ready to wing their way northward again.

Opposite page: Monarchs are strong fliers, reaching speeds of about 10 to 30 miles (16 to 48 kilometers) an hour.

Stay-at-home Monarchs

Not all Monarchs migrate. Some have short lives and don't have time to go far from the place where they hatched.

The length of a Monarch's life depends on when it is born. Those butterflies emerging in spring and early summer have short lives. They *mate,* or come together to produce young, within about four days after their hatching. They live for only about a month after that. During that time, the females lay their eggs.

It is the Monarchs that emerge in late summer or autumn that live long enough to migrate. Born in cooler weather, their growth is slowed down. And as autumn temperatures keep dropping, they naturally head for a warmer climate. They don't have time for mating and laying eggs. For those Monarchs, producing the next generation of butterflies will come later.

At night and in cool weather, Monarchs rest on trees or bushes. They can't fly when the temperature drops below 55 degrees Fahrenheit (13 degrees Celsius).

44

Northward Bound

For those Monarchs that have migrated, mating takes place before they leave their southern wintering grounds or on the journey back north. The butterflies don't stay together after they mate. Instead, they slowly head north, alone or in small groups. Along the way, some of the females stop to lay their eggs. In the next four to six weeks, these eggs will go through their transformation from egg to caterpillar to pupa to adult butterfly. By instinct, the new butterflies know that they must continue north, and they know when they've reached their summer home.

Not all of the butterflies that start the journey will finish it. Many are eaten by predators. Others die on the long, hard flight north. But there are always new butterflies hatching to take their place in the great northward migration. And there are always new butterflies hatching in time for another great Monarch migration in the fall to their southern wintering grounds.

Words To Know

Antennae   Long sensitive feelers located between a butterfly's eyes.

Caterpillar   The second stage in a Monarch's life. Also called the larva.

Chrysalis   The hard case that covers the pupa.

Claspers   The grasping hooklike claws that a caterpillar uses to hold onto a leaf.

Filaments   Dark, threadlike structures on a caterpillar's head and tail.

Instinct   A strong inborn urge or behavior pattern.

Larva   The caterpillar stage of a butterfly's life.

Lens   One part of an insect's eye that helps it to see objects.

Mate   To come together to produce young.

Migrate   To travel from one place to another at different seasons for food, a better climate, or raising young.

Molt   To shed a layer of skin.

Nectar   The sweet liquid produced by plants and used as food by some insects.

Predator   An animal that hunts other animals for food.

Proboscis   A butterfly's hollow, strawlike drinking tube that is used to suck nectar from flowers.

Pupa   The stage in a butterfly's life before it turns into an adult.

Spinneret   A body part in a caterpillar's mouth that is used to spin silky threads.

Spiracles   Breathing holes on the sides of a caterpillar's body.

Index

PHOTO CREDITS
Cover: Bill Ivy. **Interiors:** Bill Ivy, 4, 8, 11, 12, 16, 19, 20, 22, 24, 27, 29, 30, 33, 39. */Eco-Art Productions:* Norman Lightfoot, 7, 14. */Valan Photos:* Herman H. Giethoorn, 34. */Ivy Images:* J.D. Taylor, 37; Leonard Rue Enterprises, 41. /Fred Bruemmer, 42. */Spectrum Stock:* Mark Newman, 45.

Getting To Know...

Nature's Children

Walruses

Laima Dingwall

SCHOLASTIC INC.

New York Toronto London Auckland Sydney
Mexico City New Delhi Hong Kong Buenos Aires

Facts in Brief

Classification of the Walrus

      Class: *Mammalia* (mammals)

      Order: *Pinnipedia* (pinnipeds)

      Family: *Odobenidae*

      Genus: *Rosmarus*

      Species: *Rosmarus divergens* (Pacific Walrus)

                   Rosmarus rosmarus (Atlantic Walrus)

World distribution. Found all around the edges of the Arctic ice cap and in coastal areas as far south as Labrador.

Habitat. Shallow seas; ice packs; rocky coasts.

Distinctive physical characteristics. Downward-curving tusks; flippers; mustaches; thick layer of blubber under leathery skin.

Habits. Lives in herds; migrates in a regular pattern; feeds in the morning.

Diet. Primarily mollusks, supplemented by other small sea-bottom dwellers such as annelids and crustacea.

Published by Scholastic Inc.
90 Old Sherman Turnpike, Danbury, Connecticut 06816.

SCHOLASTIC and associated logos are trademarks and/or registered trademarks of Scholastic Inc.

ISBN: 0-7172-6065-8   Printed in the U.S.A.

Edited by: Elizabeth Grace Zuraw   *Photo Editor:* Nancy Norton
Photo Rights: Ivy Images   *Cover Design:* Niemand Design

Have you ever wondered . . .

Most people can't help but smile when they see a walrus. Maybe the walrus's comical face, complete with a bristly mustache, is what does it. Or maybe it's the friendly way the walrus has of snuggling up to its neighbors on the ice.

But however amusing the walrus can be, there's far more to this sea animal than first meets the eye. If you could visit the Arctic coast where the walrus lives, you'd see that this big, funny-looking animal is truly a superb cold-weather survivor. Let's take a closer look at how the walrus lives.

The coarse whiskers on its muzzle are about the only hair a walrus has.

Meet the Family

If the walrus held a family reunion for its North American relatives, who would come? Its cousins the sea lion and the seal, of course.

The walrus and its relatives belong to a group of animals called *pinnipeds,* a word that means "flipper feet." Because pinnipeds spend much of their time swimming in the ocean, *flippers*—wide flat limbs—are much more useful to them than ordinary legs would be.

Although walruses and their relatives are sea-living animals, they're not at all like fish. Fish breathe through gills and spend all of their life underwater. Walruses, on the other hand, have lungs, just as you do, and must come to the surface to breathe air. Furthermore, fish are cold-blooded, whereas walruses are warm-blooded. Animals are *cold-blooded* if they take on the temperature of the water and air around them. Warm-blooded walruses, just as you, have a body temperature that stays more or less the same all the time.

Walruses may need to come up for air periodically, but when they're in the water they're excellent swimmers and divers.

What Big Teeth You Have

It's easy to tell walruses from their relatives. They're the only ones with *tusks,* two very long pointed teeth, one at each corner of the mouth. The tusks start growing soon after a walrus is born. By the time the walrus is two years old, its tusks are 4 inches (10 centimeters) long. An adult male walrus might have tusks as long as 3 feet (1 meter), each weighing almost as much as a good-sized watermelon. Of course, you can't see all of a walrus's tusks. Parts of them are hidden inside its mouth.

A female walrus's tusks are shorter, narrower, and more curved than a male's.

Male tusks

Female tusks

The size of a male's tusks is important. In any argument with other males, the animal with the longest tusks usually gets his way.

All-purpose Tusks

In addition to its tusks, the walrus has 16 other teeth, all of which are quite small. Why are its tusks so large? Because they have several uses.

Male walruses use their tusks when they have to fight other males to show their strength. And walruses use their tusks in self-defense. Because tusks are strong and almost impossible to break, they make fierce weapons. Walruses use them to defend themselves against the Polar Bear and Killer Whale, two of their most dangerous predators. A *predator* is an animal that hunts other animals for food.

Tusks also make handy grappling hooks when a walrus wants to climb out of the water onto a slippery ice floe. The walrus simply stabs its tusks into the ice and hoists itself over the edge. Tusks are helpful for getting around on land, too. The walrus uses its tusks like ski poles, sticking them into the ice or snow and pulling itself along. Or sometimes a walrus uses its tusks just to prop its head up!

A walrus can use its tusks the way a mountain climber uses a pick. Scientists once believed that the walrus used its tusks to dig for food, but that theory has been disproved.

Walruses East and West

Two kinds of walruses live in North America: the Pacific Walrus and the Atlantic Walrus.

The Pacific Walrus lives on the western edge of the Arctic Ocean, near Alaska. The Atlantic Walrus makes its home on the eastern edge of the Arctic Ocean, near Hudson Bay and Labrador.

Opposite page: *Walruses spend a good deal of time out of the water, resting and sunbathing on ice floes and beaches.*

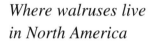

Where walruses live in North America

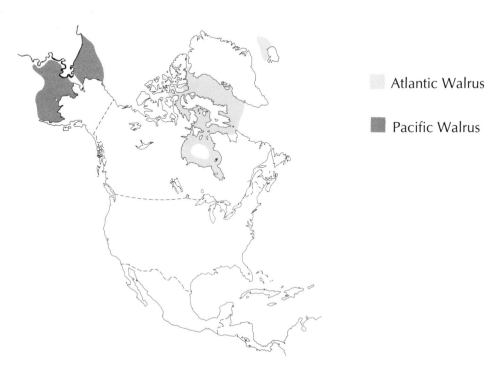

Atlantic Walrus

Pacific Walrus

As Big as a...Walrus!

The French explorer Jacques Cartier saw walruses on his early voyages to North America. When he later wrote about them, he called them "great beasts...like large oxen."

No wonder he said that. The walrus is HUGE. A full-grown male Pacific Walrus weighs 2,400 pounds (1,100 kilograms) or more. And from the tips of its whiskers to the end of its tail, it might be as long as 13 feet (4 meters). In other words, a walrus can weigh about as much as 14 full-grown adult men and be as long as a large car!

The Atlantic Walrus is slightly smaller. It weighs an average of 2,000 pounds (900 kilograms) and measures about 10 feet (3 meters) long.

A walrus's considerable bulk is covered by wrinkled skin that's up to 2 inches (about 5 centimeters) thick. The skin normally has many lumps, folds, creases, and small bumps.

Walruses Love Water

Everything about the walrus is suited to life in the water. Doesn't even the shape of the walrus's body remind you of an oversized fish? That streamlined form helps the walrus cut through the water easily and quickly.

You could be excused for not noticing the walrus's ears. They're small slits on the sides of its head. When the walrus dives underwater, a flap of skin automatically closes over each ear to keep out water. And the walrus doesn't need to worry about getting water up its nose either. A fold of skin covers its nostrils when it dives, just like built-in nose plugs.

Today's water-loving walruses trace their ancestry to bear-like creatures that existed as far back as 20 million years ago.

Cold-water Comfort

You might find swimming in cold Arctic water a chilling experience. Not the walrus. Its tough leathery skin covers a layer—up to 6 inches (15 centimeters) thick—of special fat called *blubber*. Blubber is like a snugly parka for the walrus. It keeps the walrus warm not only in icy water but also in chilly air.

The walrus's large, flat head is particularly useful when it's swimming under the ice. If the walrus needs to come to the surface for a breath of air, it uses its head as a battering ram to make a hole in the ice. You might say "Ouch!" but the walrus's sturdy head isn't hurt by such an impact.

The walrus rests at sea in a vertical position. Two inflatable air sacs, or pouches, in its neck keep its bulky head above water.

Walrus Underwater

The walrus has two pairs of flippers—one near the front of its body and another pair in the back. Its front flippers have fine long "fingers" joined by webs of skin. When the walrus spreads these fingers, the flippers become wide, powerful paddles with lots of swimming power.

The walrus uses its rear flippers like the rudder on a boat. They help the walrus change directions when it's in the water.

Walrus flipper

A walrus's layer of blubber not only keeps it warm, it helps the animal float.

Dive, Dive, Dive

The walrus dives underwater to find food and to escape predators. It usually finds its food in shallow water close to shore, but it can dive as deep as 300 feet (91 meters). And it can stay underwater for as long as 15 minutes without coming up for air!

How does the walrus do it? After all, walruses don't breathe through gills as fish do. They have lungs, so they need air.

When a walrus is underwater, its muscles relax and its heart rate slows down. That way it uses up the supply of air in its lungs slowly. This allows the walrus to stay underwater for a long time.

The walrus is a very graceful swimmer—and a fast one. It can reach speeds of up to 15 miles (24 kilometers) per hour in the water. That's about five times the speed of the fastest human swimmer!

Because walruses feed at the bottom of bodies of water, they prefer shallow areas less than 60 feet (18 meters) deep.

Walruses sometimes lie about in shallow water and wait
for the incoming tide to lift them up onto a rocky ledge.

Thump, Thump, Thump

The walrus may be graceful in the water, but on land—that's a different story. There it bumps along like an overgrown caterpillar.

The walrus uses its short, but very sturdy, flippers to push itself along the ground. It can swing its back flippers forward and fan them out to brace itself. This way, the walrus can push itself up and forward with a lunging thump. And if a walrus is on an ice flow and in a hurry, it hooks its tusks into the ice and pulls itself forward.

The walrus may look clumsy and comical as it waddles and thumps along, but it can reach surprising speeds when it's pursuing an intruder or escaping danger.

Ask a Walrus to Dinner

Opposite page:
A sensitive mustache and muzzle are the walrus's main tools in its search for food.

A walrus will eat almost any small creatures it can find on the sea bottom. It often eats shrimps, whelks, marine worms, and sea cucumbers. But its favorite food, and the mainstay of its diet, is clams.

How does a walrus find clams in the sand on the ocean's bottom? Scientists once believed that the walrus raked along the bottom with its tusks to pry clams loose. Now researchers have evidence that a walrus uses only its bristly mustache.

A walrus's mustache is made up of some 400 very stiff, thick, strong hairs arranged in neat rows. Each hair is tipped with sensitive nerves. That kind of mustache is like having 400 extra fingers to help you find food!

The walrus is a very delicate eater. It can eat clams without swallowing any part of the shell. No one has ever figured out how it can do this. Somehow the walrus just sucks the soft clam meat right out of the shell, using its tongue and thick, rubbery lips.

26

Wall-to-Wall Walrus

After a good feed, a walrus usually likes to haul itself out of the water to rest or snooze in the sun. A group of walruses often has its own favorite *oogli.* That's the name that the *Inuit,* or Eskimo peoples, have given to the place where walruses gather. An oogli can be a rocky beach or nothing more than a large ice floe surrounded by deep water.

No matter what or where the oogli is, one thing is sure. The oogli is always crowded with walruses. In fact, sometimes so many walruses snuggle so closely together that it's hard to tell where one walrus ends and another begins. Together they look like one giant walrus carpet!

Walruses like being with each other, and often haul out in huge groups on ice floes or rocky islands.

Warring Walruses

With so many walruses gathered together on the same oogli, it's not surprising that clashes occur. At times, walruses fight so loudly that their calls can be heard 1.5 miles (2 kilometers) away!

What do walruses fight about? Perhaps one walrus has rolled over and accidentally jabbed another one with its tusks. Or a walrus might fancy sleeping in another walrus's cozy spot.

Sometimes serious confrontations take place. Two walruses will face one another, rear up on their flippers, and throw their heads back to threaten each other with their tusks. But such fights rarely come to blows. The walrus with the shorter tusks usually gives way. Soon all the walruses relax and lie quietly together again—until the next squabble.

Tusks are important in settling walrus confrontations.
The animal with the longest tusks usually gets its way.

In the Pink

When a walrus hauls itself out of the water onto an oogli, its thick, leathery skin is quite pale and gray. But after the animal has stretched out in the sun for a few minutes, its skin slowly turns a rosy shade of pink.

No, the walrus isn't getting sun-burned! It's just that the blood vessels under the animal's skin expand in the warm sun. Blood rushes into the vessels, giving the walrus's skin a rosy color. While the walrus was down in the icy water, its blood flowed deep into its body to support its internal organs. As the blood flowed away from the walrus's body surface, the animal's skin lost its rosy color and turned gray.

It's not magic! Cozily on land after a chilly swim, the walrus's skin changes from dull gray to rosy pink.

The More the Merrier

A lone walrus is a sad walrus. Walruses are very social animals and love nothing more than the company of their own kind.

Walruses live and travel in groups. There might be a hundred or more walruses in a group, all mixed together, old and young, male and female. Female walruses are called *cows,* and the males are *bulls.* If you guessed that a young walrus is called a *calf,* you're right. During *mating season,* the time of year during which animals come together to produce young, the older bulls drive away the younger ones. The young males sometimes form their own groups and stay on the edge of the main group.

Walruses sometimes form herds of up to 2,000 bulls, cows, and calves.

Walrus on the Move

A walrus spends the summer months in the waters along the edge of the Arctic ice. The Pacific Walrus summers along the northern coasts of Siberia and Alaska. Its Atlantic cousin spends summers on the edge of the Atlantic Arctic.

Come winter, when the northernmost seas start to freeze over, both the Pacific and Atlantic Walruses travel south. They *migrate,* or travel, to places where the warmer currents and shallower waters keep the ice from closing up the bays and the sea. Sometimes they might do a little ice-hitchhiking. If the big ice floes are heading in the right direction, the walruses drift along with them.

Once spring rolls around, the walrus travels north again.

When migrating, walruses like to hitch a ride on ice. But if the ice floe heads off in the wrong direction, it's time for the walruses to start swimming!

Mating Time

Opposite page:
A female walrus is ready to start a family at about 6 or 7 years of age. Males don't fully mature until they're about 15 years old.

After their springtime migration to the far north, it's time for the walruses to mate. First, each male walrus stakes out a territory on an ice floe. A *territory* is an area that an animal lives in and defends from other animals of the same kind.

A male walrus mates with as many as 30 females in a season. A female walrus, however, usually mates with only one male. All the females that the male has mated with crowd into the territory he has claimed. He guards these females and fights off any other bulls that try to come near.

Once mating season is over, the bulls no longer are concerned about their territories or about the other males. In fact, they don't even worry about the females that they have just been so fiercely protecting. The females have to raise their young with no help from the fathers.

Walrus Birthday Time

About a year after mating, a female walrus is ready to give birth. If possible, she uses an ice floe near the oogli as her nursery. Usually only one baby is born. Twins are very rare. At birth, a baby walrus is tiny—at least by walrus standards. The newborn weighs from 100 to 150 pounds (45 to 68 kilograms). That's about as heavy as most full-grown women!

A newborn walrus is weak and helpless. Its layer of blubber is very thin, and it has a coat of only short, silvery gray baby hair to protect it from the cold. It's not surprising that walrus babies spend much of their time trying to keep warm by cuddling close to their mothers.

As a baby walrus snuggles next to its mother, it *nurses* often—it drinks the thick, creamy milk in its mother's body. The young walrus will drink this rich milk until it's almost 2 years old.

Opposite page: *A walrus mother and baby are seldom apart, whether on ice or land or in the water. When the mother dives for food, she often clasps the calf in her flippers and takes it along.*

A calf stays with its mother and nurses until it's two years old. By then it's able to find food by itself.

Walrus Motherhood

The female walrus is an excellent mother. In fact, she'll sometimes even adopt an orphaned baby walrus and raise it as her own.

The mother walrus and her baby are very affectionate. They spend much of their time giving each other tiny "kisses" by rubbing their bristly mustaches. They even give each other walrus hugs, and the mother sometimes holds her baby with her flippers.

A mother walrus tries never to let her baby wander out of her sight. If a baby should get separated from its mother, it cries so loudly that she'll soon come to the rescue.

A young walrus can swim soon after it's born. Often it swims side by side with its mother, but sometimes it has a hard time keeping up. When that happens, the baby climbs onto its mother's back and holds her sides tightly with its flippers. Sometimes it will hitchhike a ride this way for hours.

Overleaf:
It's easy to see: With skin up to 2 inches (about 5 centimeters) thick, and about a 6-inch (15-centimeter) layer of blubber, the stout walrus is built for life in the icy Arctic.

Time To Leave Mother

A young walrus is usually safe as long as its mother is nearby. She protects it and teaches it how to find its own food and how to avoid Polar Bears, Killer Whales, and other enemies of young walruses. After two years, it's time for the mother to give birth to a new baby and for the young walrus to make a life of its own.

The young walrus sunning itself on the oogli probably has a long happy life ahead of it. It can go clam-digging, enjoy cold-water swims, and snuggle with other walruses for many years to come. Some walruses live for as long as 40 years.

Words To Know

Blood Vessels Tubes, arteries, and veins through which blood flows in the body.

Blubber A layer of fat on an animal's body that keeps the cold out and body heat in.

Bull A male walrus.

Calf A baby walrus.

Cold-blooded Having a body temperature that's controlled by the temperature of the surrounding air or water.

Cow A female walrus.

Flippers Wide flat limbs adapted specially for swimming.

Inuit The Eskimo peoples of North America.

Lungs Parts of the body that take in air and put it into the blood.

Mate To come together to produce young.

Migration A seasonal journey to find food, a suitable climate to live, or a place to mate and bear young.

Nurse To drink milk from a mother's body.

Oogli The Inuit word for a walrus gathering place.

Pinnipeds A group of animals that have flippers.

Predator An animal that hunts other animals for food.

Sac A pouch-like structure.

Territory The area that an animal or group of animals lives in and often defends from other animals of the same kind.

Tusks Two elongated, pointed teeth that extend outside the walrus's mouth.

Index

PHOTO CREDITS

Cover: H. Kalen, *Ivy Images.* **Interiors:** Leonard Lee Rue III, 4, 19. */Thomas Stack & Associates:* Thomas Kitchin, 7. */Valan Photos:* Stephen J. Krasemann, 8, 12, 17, 27, 28, 35, 36. /Wayne Lynch, 11, 23, 39. */Visuals Unlimited:* Tom J. Ulrich, 15. */Canada In Stock/Ivy Images:* H. Kiliaan, 24; Gary Crandall, 31. /Fred Bruemmer, 21, 32-33, 40, 42, 44-45